Before You Begin

Most of the sample doorstops shown here are constructed as stitched plastic canvas boxes that encase a standard masonry brick for weight.

Before cutting the plastic canvas for your doorstop's top, bottom, front, back and sides, compare your brick against the dimensions given for the finished project. If your brick is larger or smaller, adjust the size of the plastic canvas pieces accordingly. You will find it a simple matter to extend the stitching pattern to fill the plastic canvas pieces.

Or choose an alternative source for the weight—a doubled freezer-weight plastic bag filled with clean gravel, river stones, aquarium gravel, sand, dry beans or rice.

Cottage

Design by Michele Wilcox

Size: 8⅛ inches W x 5⅛ inches H x 2¼ inches D (20.7cm x 13cm x 5.7cm)
Skill Level: Beginner

Materials

- 1⅓ sheets clear 7-count plastic canvas
- Uniek Needloft plastic canvas yarn as listed in color key
- DMC #3 pearl cotton as listed in color key
- Brick or other weight
- #16 tapestry needle
- Hot-glue gun

Stitching Step by Step

1 Cut cottage motif, left fence, right fence, two front/back pieces, two top/bottom pieces and two sides from 7-count plastic canvas according to graphs.

2 Overcast fences with white. Stitch remaining plastic canvas pieces according to graphs, filling in uncoded area on cottage motif with forest Continental Stitches.

3 Overcast cottage motif using adjacent colors. Using black #3 pearl cotton, work French Knot doorknob on cottage, wrapping pearl cotton once around needle.

4 Using royal yarn through step 6, Whipstitch front and back to sides at corners; Whipstitch top to front, back and sides.

5 Insert brick or other weight. Whipstitch bottom to front, back and sides.

6 Referring to photo throughout, glue cottage motif to doorstop with bottom edges even. Glue fence sections to cottage motif.

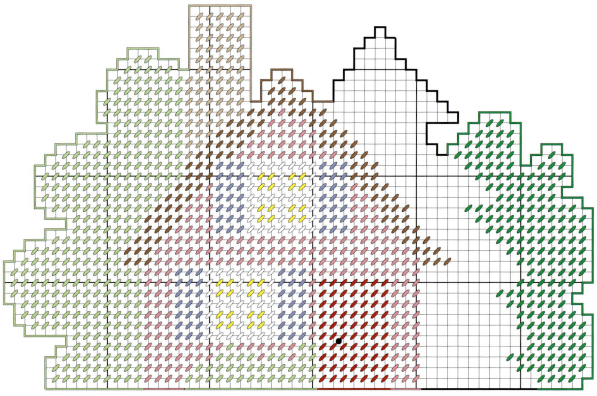

Cottage Motif
57 holes x 36 holes
Cut 1

COLOR KEY		
Yards	**Plastic Canvas Yarn**	
1 (1m)	■	Red #01
7 (6.5m)	■	Lavender #05
2 (1.9m)	■	Rust #09
4 (3.7m)	■	Cinnamon #14
7 (6.5m)	■	Fern #23
60 (54.9m)	■	Royal #32
9 (8.3m)	□	White #41
6 (5.5m)	■	Mermaid #53
2 (1.9m)	■	Yellow #57
7 (6.5m)		Uncoded area is forest #29 Continental Stitches
	╱	Forest #29 Overcast
	#3 Pearl Cotton	
1 (1m)	●	Black #310 (1-wrap) French Knot

Color numbers given are for Uniek Needloft plastic canvas yarn and DMC #3 pearl cotton.

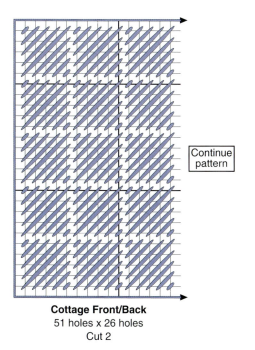

Cottage Front/Back
51 holes x 26 holes
Cut 2

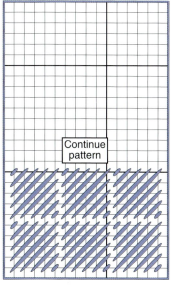

Cottage Side
16 holes x 26 holes
Cut 2

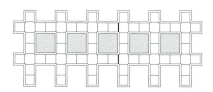

Cottage Right Fence
18 holes x 7 holes
Cut 1, cutting away gray areas

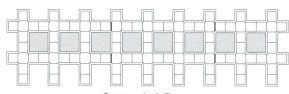

Cottage Left Fence
27 holes x 7 holes
Cut 1, cutting away gray areas

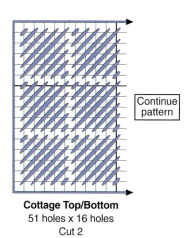

Cottage Top/Bottom
51 holes x 16 holes
Cut 2

Beach

Design by Phyllis Dobbs

Size: 8¼ inches W x 7 inches H x 2¼ inches D (21cm x 17.9cm x 5.7cm)
Skill Level: Beginner

Materials

- 2 sheets clear 7-count plastic canvas
- Uniek Needloft plastic canvas yarn as listed in color key
- 4 (3mm) black pompoms
- Brick or other weight
- #16 tapestry needle
- Hot-glue gun

Stitching Step by Step

1 Cut umbrella, sun, palm tree, front, left side and right side from plastic canvas according to graphs. Also cut one piece 58 holes x 28 holes for back and two pieces 58 holes x 16 holes for top and bottom.

2 Stitch umbrella, sun, palm tree, front and sides according to graphs, filling in uncoded areas with sail blue Continental Stitches. Fill in back and top with sail blue Continental Stitches; fill in bottom with turquoise Continental Stitches.

3 Overcast umbrella, sun and palm tree using adjacent colors.

4 Using colors adjacent to sides, Whipstitch front and back to sides at corners. Using sail blue, Whipstitch top to front, back and sides.

5 Insert brick or other weight. Using adjacent colors, Whipstitch bottom to front, back and sides.

6 Referring to photo throughout, glue umbrella, sun and palm tree to doorstop. Glue two pompoms to each crab for eyes.

COLOR KEY

Yards	Plastic Canvas Yarn
6 (5.5m)	■ Christmas red #02
2 (1.9m)	■ Maple #13
8 (7.4m)	■ Holly #27
1 (1m)	■ Forest #29
2 (1.9m)	■ Royal #32
2 (1.9m)	■ Baby blue #36
14 (12.2m)	■ Eggshell #39
1 (1m)	□ White #41
30 (27.5m)	■ Turquoise #54
5 (4.6m)	■ Yellow #57
50 (45.8m)	Uncoded areas are sail blue #35 Continental Stitches
	╱ Sail blue #35 Whipstitch

Color numbers given are for Uniek Needloft plastic canvas yarn.

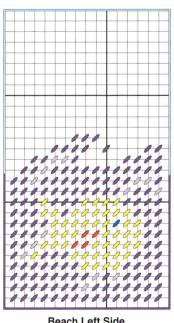

Beach Left Side
16 holes x 28 holes
Cut 1

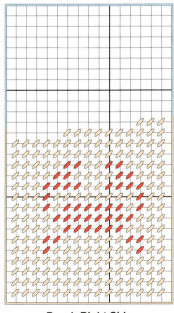

Beach Right Side
16 holes x 28 holes
Cut 1

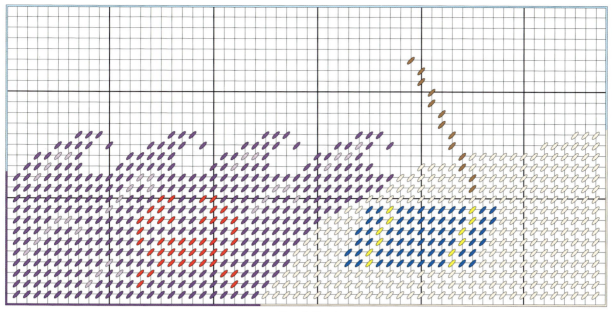

Beach Front
58 holes x 28 holes
Cut 1

Beach Palm Tree
32 holes x 41 holes
Cut 1

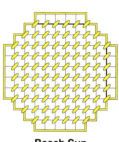

Beach Sun
11 holes x 11 holes
Cut 1

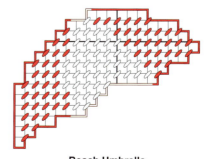

Beach Umbrella
18 holes x 13 holes
Cut 1

The Needlecraft Shop • Berne, IN 46711 • DRGnetwork.com • **Fast & Fun Doorstops 5**

Rocking Horse

Design by Phyllis Dobbs

Size: 8¼ inches W x 6⅝ inches H x 2¼ inches D
(21cm x 16.8cm x 5.7cm)
Skill Level: Beginner

Materials
- 2 sheets clear 7-count plastic canvas
- Uniek Needloft plastic canvas yarn as listed in color key
- 3mm black pompom
- Brick or other weight
- #16 tapestry needle
- Hot-glue gun

Stitching Step by Step

1 Cut rocking horse and two front/back pieces from plastic canvas according to graphs. Also cut two pieces 58 holes x 16 holes for top and bottom, and two pieces 16 holes x 28 holes for sides.

2 Stitch rocking horse, front and back according to graphs, filling in uncoded areas with sail blue Continental Stitches. Fill in top, bottom and sides with same pattern of white stitches used for front and back.

3 Overcast rocking horse according to graph.

4 Using white yarn throughout, Whipstitch front and back to sides at corners. Whipstitch top to front, back and sides.

5 Insert brick or other weight. Whipstitch bottom to front, back and sides.

6 Referring to photo, glue rocking horse to doorstop. Glue pompom to rocking horse for eye.

Rocking Horse
52 holes x 44 holes
Cut 1, cutting away gray area

COLOR KEY

Yards	Plastic Canvas Yarn
11 (10.1m)	▨ Pink #07
1 (1m)	▨ Lemon #20
90 (82.3m)	▢ White #41
5 (4.6m)	▨ Mermaid #53
12 (11m)	Uncoded areas are sail blue #35 Continental Stitches
	╱ Sail blue #35 Overcast
	● Attach pompom

Color numbers given are for Uniek Needloft plastic canvas yarn.

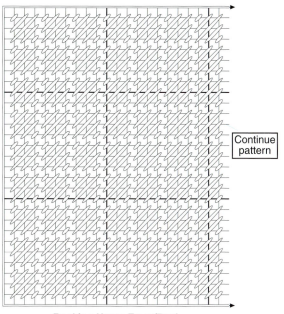

Rocking Horse Front/Back
58 holes x 28 holes
Cut 2

Sunflower

Design by Phyllis Dobbs

Size: 4 inches W x 9¼ inches H x 2¼ inches D
(10.2cm x 23.5cm x 5.7cm)
Skill Level: Beginner

Materials

- 2 sheets clear 7-count plastic canvas
- Uniek Needloft plastic canvas yarn as listed in color key
- Brick or other weight
- #16 tapestry needle
- Hot-glue gun

Stitching Step by Step

1 Cut sunflower and front from plastic canvas according to graphs. Also cut one piece 28 holes x 58 holes for back, two pieces 28 holes x 16 holes for top and bottom, and two pieces 16 holes x 58 holes for sides.

2 Stitch sunflower and front according to graphs, filling in uncoded areas with white Continental Stitches. Fill in back, top, bottom and sides with white Continental Stitches.

3 Overcast sunflower with lemon.

4 Using white yarn throughout, Whipstitch front and back to sides at corners. Whipstitch top to front, back and sides.

5 Insert brick or other weight. Whipstitch bottom to front, back and sides.

6 Glue sunflower to doorstop.

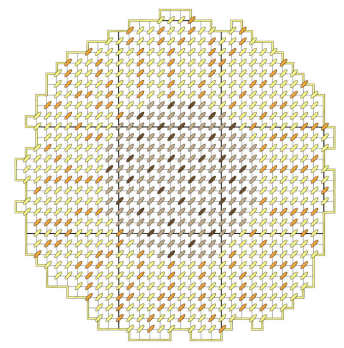

Sunflower
31 holes x 31 holes
Cut 1

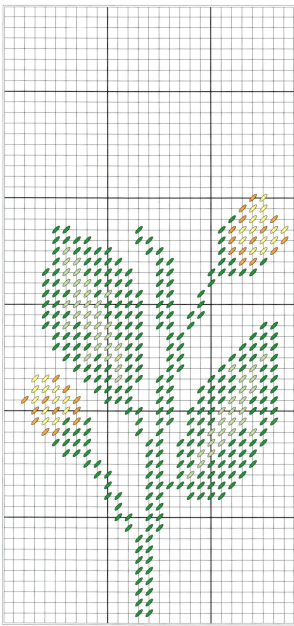

Sunflower Front
28 holes x 58 holes
Cut 1

COLOR KEY	
Yards	**Plastic Canvas Yarn**
5 (4.6m)	■ Tangerine #11
4 (3.7m)	■ Maple #13
1 (1m)	■ Cinnamon #14
12 (11m)	■ Lemon #20
3 (2.8m)	■ Fern #23
7 (6.5m)	■ Holly #27
90 (82.3m)	Uncoded areas are white #41 Continental Stitches
	╱ White #41 Whipstitch
Color numbers given are for Uniek Needloft plastic canvas yarn.	

The Needlecraft Shop • Berne, IN 46711 • DRGnetwork.com • **Fast & Fun Doorstops 9**

Clever Cat

Design by Michele Wilcox

Size: 7¼ inches W x 9¼ inches H x 2¼ inches D
(18.4cm x 23.5cm x 5.7cm)
Skill Level: Beginner

Materials

- 2 sheets clear 7-count plastic canvas
- Uniek Needloft plastic canvas yarn as listed in color key
- DMC #3 pearl cotton as listed in color key
- Brick or other weight
- #16 tapestry needle
- Hot-glue gun

Stitching Step by Step

1 Cut cat, left arm, right arm, two front/back pieces, two top/bottom pieces and two sides from plastic canvas according to graphs.

2 Stitch plastic canvas according to graphs, filling in uncoded areas with black Continental Stitches. Overcast cat and cat's arms according to graphs.

3 *Work embroidery stitches on cat using #3 pearl cotton:* Work black French Knot eye on bird and blue French Knot eyes and red French Knot nose on cat, wrapping pearl cotton once around needle. Backstitch mouth using red.

4 Using yellow yarn throughout, Whipstitch front and back to sides at corners. Whipstitch top to front, back and sides.

5 Insert brick or other weight. Whipstitch bottom to front, back and sides.

6 Referring to photo, glue arms to reverse side of cat. Glue cat to doorstop with bottom edges even.

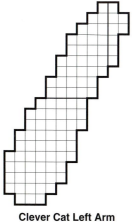

Clever Cat Left Arm
12 holes x 19 holes
Cut 1

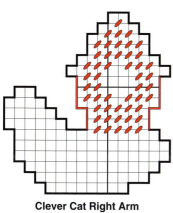

Clever Cat Right Arm
16 holes x 17 holes
Cut 1

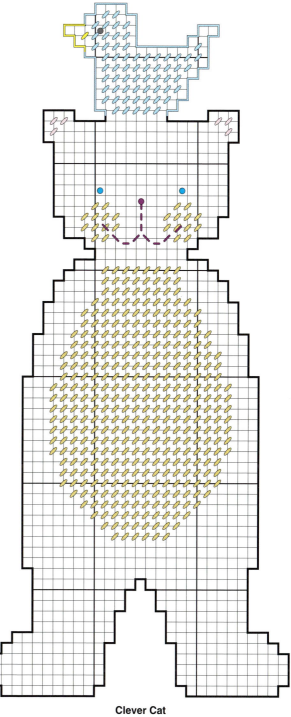

Clever Cat
29 holes x 65 holes
Cut 1

COLOR KEY

Yards	Plastic Canvas Yarn
1 (1m)	■ Red #01
1 (1m)	■ Pink #07
2 (1.8m)	■ Sail blue #35
6 (5.5m)	■ Eggshell #39
36 (33m)	■ Mermaid #53
40 (36.6m)	■ Yellow #57
20 (18.3m)	Uncoded areas are black #00 Continental Stitches
	╱ Black #00 Overcast
	#3 Pearl Cotton
1 (1m)	╱ Red #666 Backstitch
	● Red #666 (1-wrap) French Knot
1 (1m)	● Blue #798 (1-wrap) French Knot
1 (1m)	● Black #310 (1-wrap) French Knot

Color numbers given are for Uniek Needloft plastic canvas yarn and DMC #3 pearl cotton.

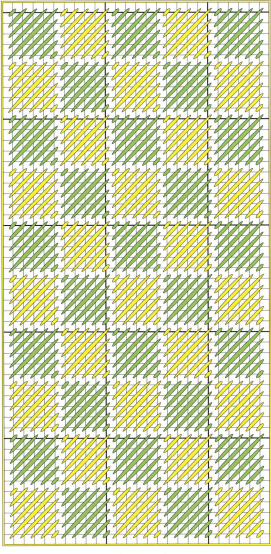

Clever Cat Front/Back
26 holes x 51 holes
Cut 2

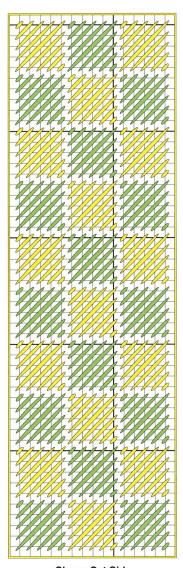

Clever Cat Side
16 holes x 51 holes
Cut 2

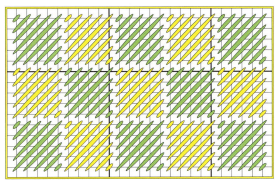

Clever Cat Top/Bottom
26 holes x 16 holes
Cut 2

COLOR KEY		
Yards	**Plastic Canvas Yarn**	
1 (1m)	■	Red #01
1 (1m)	■	Pink #07
2 (1.8m)	■	Sail blue #35
6 (5.5m)	■	Eggshell #39
36 (33m)	■	Mermaid #53
40 (36.6m)	■	Yellow #57
20 (18.3m)		Uncoded areas are black #00 Continental Stitches
	╱	Black #00 Overcast
	#3 Pearl Cotton	
1 (1m)	╱	Red #666 Backstitch
	●	Red #666 (1-wrap) French Knot
1 (1m)	●	Blue #798 (1-wrap) French Knot
1 (1m)	●	Black #310 (1-wrap) French Knot

Color numbers given are for Uniek Needloft plastic canvas yarn and DMC #3 pearl cotton.

Fresh Eggs

Design by Celia Lange Designs

Size: 7 inches W x 8¼ inches H x 3⅞ inches D (17.8cm x 21cm x 9.8cm) excluding handle
Skill Level: Beginner

Materials

- ❑ 2 sheets Darice Ultra Stiff 7-count plastic canvas
- ❑ Red Heart Classic Art. E267 medium weight yarn as listed in color key
- ❑ Red Heart Super Saver Art. E300 and Art. 301 medium weight yarn as listed in color key
- ❑ DMC 6-strand embroidery floss as listed in color key
- ❑ 2 (2-inch x 1-inch/5.1cm x 2.5cm) strips blue craft foam
- ❑ Yellow plastic-covered wire coat hanger
- ❑ Floral clay
- ❑ Plastic wrap
- ❑ Tan shredded-paper filler
- ❑ Artificial eggs
- ❑ Wire cutters
- ❑ #16 tapestry needle
- ❑ Hot-glue gun

Stitching Step by Step

1 Cut hen, wing, nest, two basket handles, two front/back pieces, one bottom and two sides from plastic canvas according to graphs.

2 Stitch hen, wing, nest, handles, front, bottom and sides according to graphs, filling in uncoded areas on hen and wing with bronze Continental Stitches. Stitch back as for front, omitting lettering.

3 Overcast hen, wing and nest according to graphs. Using 6 strands black embroidery floss, work French Knot eye on hen, wrapping floss once around needle.

4 Using skipper blue yarn through step 5, Whipstitch front, back and sides to bottom and to each other at corners. Overcast top edges. Overcast short ends of handles.

5 *Handle:* Using wire cutters, cut a 16-inch (40.6cm) piece from coat hanger. Referring to photo throughout, bend hanger to fit inside basket. Sandwich stitched plastic canvas handles around wire at top of basket; Whipstitch long edges together, enclosing hanger. Glue wire ends inside basket; glue strips of craft foam over wire ends.

6 Glue hen, nest and wing to front, keeping bottom edges of nest and front even.

7 Shape floral clay in a block to fit in bottom of basket; wrap in plastic wrap and glue in bottom of basket.

8 Fill basket with shredded-paper filler and artificial eggs.

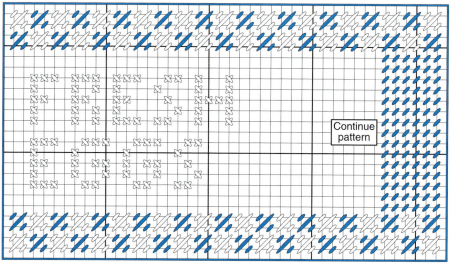

Fresh Eggs Front/Back
43 holes x 24 holes
Cut 2
Stitch front as graphed
Stitch back omitting letters

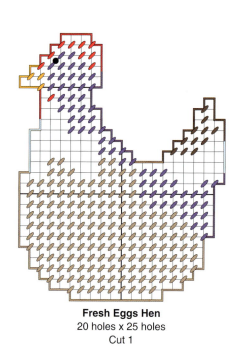

Fresh Eggs Hen
20 holes x 25 holes
Cut 1

Fresh Eggs Wing
15 holes x 10 holes
Cut 1

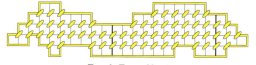

Fresh Eggs Nest
23 holes x 5 holes
Cut 1

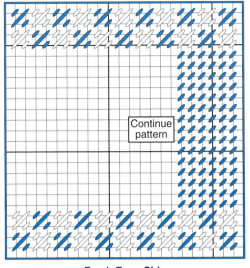

Fresh Eggs Side
23 holes x 24 holes
Cut 2

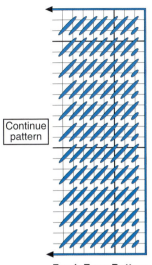

Fresh Eggs Bottom
43 holes x 23 holes
Cut 1

Fresh Eggs Handle
19 holes x 5 holes
Cut 2

COLOR KEY	
Yards	**Medium Weight Yarn**
8 (7.4m)	☐ Off-white #3
1 (1m)	Gold #321
1 (1m)	Brown #328
5 (4.6m)	Warm brown #336
3 (2.8m)	Mid brown #339
2 (1.9m)	Honey gold #645
57 (52.1m)	■ Skipper blue #848
1 (1m)	Country red #914
2 (1.9m)	Uncoded areas on hen and wing are bronze #286 Continental Stitches
	╱ Bronze #286 Overcast
	6-Strand Embroidery Floss
	● Black #310 (1-wrap) French Knot

Color numbers given are for Red Heart Classic Art. E267 and Super Saver Art. E300 and Art. E301 medium weight yarn, and DMC 6-strand embroidery floss.

Farm Boy

Design by Michele Wilcox

Size: 6¾ inches W x 7¾ inches H x 2½ inches D
(17.2cm x 19.7cm x 6.4cm)
Skill Level: Beginner

Materials

- 1½ sheets clear 7-count plastic canvas
- Uniek Needloft plastic canvas yarn as listed in color key
- DMC #5 pearl cotton as listed in color key
- 2 light blue ½-inch (13mm) flat buttons
- Brick or other weight
- Sewing needle and blue thread
- #16 tapestry needle
- Hot-glue gun

Stitching Step by Step

1 Cut farm boy, two front/back pieces, two top/bottom pieces and two sides from plastic canvas according to graphs.

2 Stitch plastic canvas according to graphs, substituting camel for sail blue when stitching bottom and filling in uncoded areas with royal Continental Stitches. Overcast farm boy according to graph.

3 *Work embroidery stitches on farm boy using #5 pearl cotton:* Work blue French Knot eyes on crow, wrapping pearl cotton once around needle. Work black French Knot eyes on farm boy, red French Knot nose and red French Knots on patch, wrapping pearl cotton once around needle. Backstitch and Straight Stitch mouth using red. Backstitch between legs using black. Backstitch lines on shirt using green, carrying stitches over edges to reverse side as shown.

4 Using needle and thread, stitch buttons to farm boy where indicated on graph.

5 Using sail blue and camel yarn throughout as indicated on graphs, Whipstitch front and back to sides at corners. Whipstitch top to front, back and sides.

6 Insert brick or other weight. Whipstitch bottom to front, back and sides.

7 Glue farm boy to doorstop with bottom edges even.

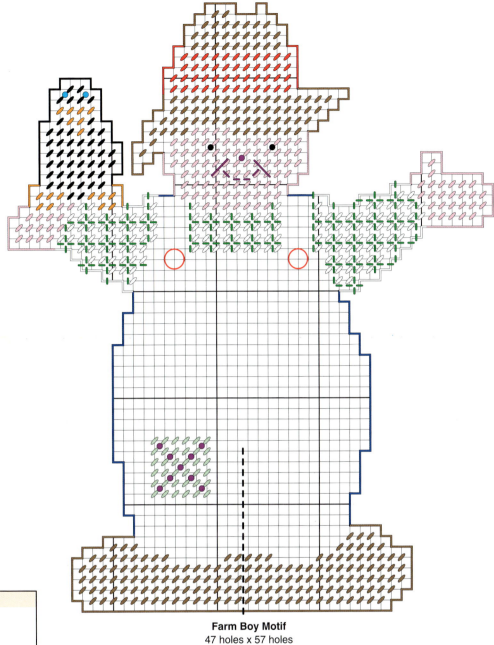

Farm Boy Motif
47 holes x 57 holes
Cut 1

COLOR KEY

Yards	Plastic Canvas Yarn
2 (1.9m)	■ Black #00
2 (1.9m)	■ Red #01
1 (1m)	■ Tangerine #11
8 (7.4m)	■ Cinnamon #14
1 (1m)	■ Fern #23
46 (42.1m)	□ Sail blue #35
4 (3.7m)	■ Beige #40
5 (4.6m)	□ White #41
36 (33m)	□ Camel #43
14 (12.9m)	Uncoded areas are royal #32 Continental Stitches
	∕ Royal #32 Overcast

#5 Pearl Cotton

3 (2.8m)	∕ Green #700 Backstitch
1 (1m)	∕ Black #310 Straight Stitch
1 (1m)	∕ Red #666 Backstitch and Straight Stitch
	● Red #666 (1-wrap) French Knot
	● Blue #798 (1-wrap) French Knot
1 (1m)	● Black #310 (1-wrap) French Knot
	○ Attach button

Color numbers given are for Uniek Needloft plastic canvas yarn and DMC #5 pearl cotton.

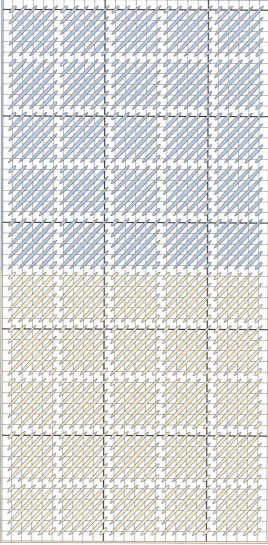

Farm Boy Front/Back
26 holes x 51 holes
Cut 2

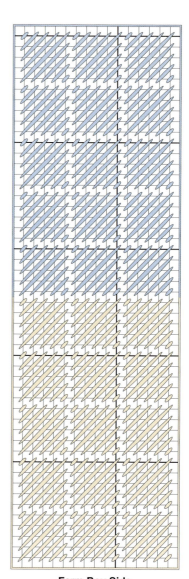

Farm Boy Side
16 holes x 51 holes
Cut 2

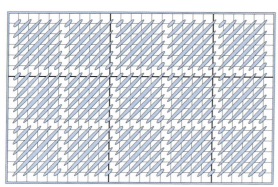

Farm Boy Top/Bottom
26 holes x 16 holes
Cut 2
Stitch 1 as graphed for top
Stitch 1 with camel for bottom

COLOR KEY		
Yards		**Plastic Canvas Yarn**
2 (1.9m)	■	Black #00
2 (1.9m)	■	Red #01
1 (1m)	■	Tangerine #11
8 (7.4m)	■	Cinnamon #14
1 (1m)	■	Fern #23
46 (42.1m)	■	Sail blue #35
4 (3.7m)	■	Beige #40
5 (4.6m)	□	White #41
36 (33m)	■	Camel #43
14 (12.9m)		Uncoded areas are royal #32 Continental Stitches
	╱	Royal #32 Overcast
		#5 Pearl Cotton
3 (2.8m)	╱	Green #700 Backstitch
1 (1m)	╱	Black #310 Straight Stitch
1 (1m)	╱	Red #666 Backstitch and Straight Stitch
	●	Red #666 (1-wrap) French Knot
1 (1m)	●	Blue #798 (1-wrap) French Knot
	●	Black #310 (1-wrap) French Knot
	○	Attach button

Color numbers given are for Uniek Needloft plastic canvas yarn and DMC #5 pearl cotton.

Santa

Design by Michele Wilcox

Size: 7¾ inches W x 5 inches H x 2½ inches D (19.7cm x 12.7cm x 6.4cm) excluding stars
Skill Level: Beginner

Materials
- 2 sheets clear 7-count plastic canvas
- 5 Uniek QuickShape 5-inch plastic canvas stars
- Uniek Needloft plastic canvas yarn as listed in color key
- DMC #5 pearl cotton as listed in color key
- 4 (9-inch/22.9cm) pieces green 22-gauge floral wire
- ⅜-inch-diameter (9mm) wooden dowel
- Brick or other weight
- #16 tapestry needle
- Hot-glue gun

Stitching Step by Step

1 Cut Santa/tree motif and two front/back pieces from 7-count plastic canvas according to graphs. Also cut two pieces 51 holes x 16 holes for top and bottom, and two pieces 16 holes x 26 holes for sides.

2 From plastic canvas stars, cut two large stars, two medium stars and one small star according to graphs, cutting away gray areas.

3 Stitch Santa/tree motif, front, back and stars according to graphs, Overcasting stars with tangerine as you stitch. Stitch top, bottom and sides in same pattern as for front and back.

4 Overcast Santa/tree motif using adjacent colors. Using black #5 pearl cotton, work French Knot eyes on Santa, wrapping pearl cotton once around needle.

5 Using royal yarn through step 6, Whipstitch front and back to sides at corners; Whipstitch top to front, back and sides.

6 Insert brick or other weight. Whipstitch bottom to front, back and sides.

7 Coil wires around dowel; slide off and extend coils as desired. Set aside one large star. Referring to photo throughout, thread a wire end through center bottom edge of each remaining star, twisting wire ends to secure. Glue other ends of wires to reverse side of Santa/tree motif as shown.

8 Glue Santa/tree motif and remaining large star to doorstop.

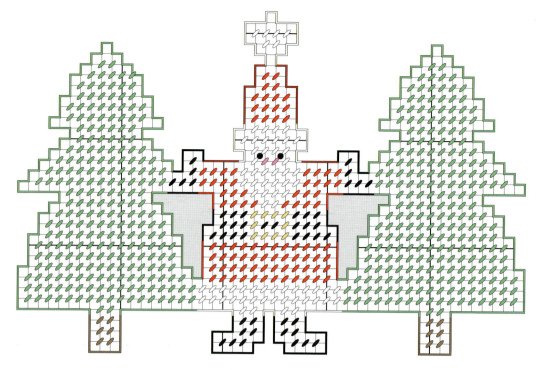

Santa/Tree Motif
49 holes x 32 holes
Cut 1, cutting away gray areas

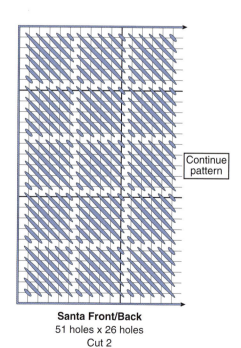

Santa Front/Back
51 holes x 26 holes
Cut 2

COLOR KEY	
Yards	**Plastic Canvas Yarn**
4 (3.7m)	■ Black #00
4 (3.7m)	■ Christmas red #02
1 (1m)	■ Pink #07
8 (7.4m)	■ Tangerine #11
13 (11.9m)	■ Fern #23
75 (68.6m)	■ Royal #32
3 (2.8m)	□ White #41
1 (1m)	■ Camel #43
	#5 Pearl Cotton
1 (1m)	● Black #310 (1-wrap) French Knot

Color numbers given are for Uniek Needloft plastic canvas yarn and DMC #5 pearl cotton.

20 Fast & Fun Doorstops • The Needlecraft Shop • Berne, IN 46711 • DRGnetwork.com

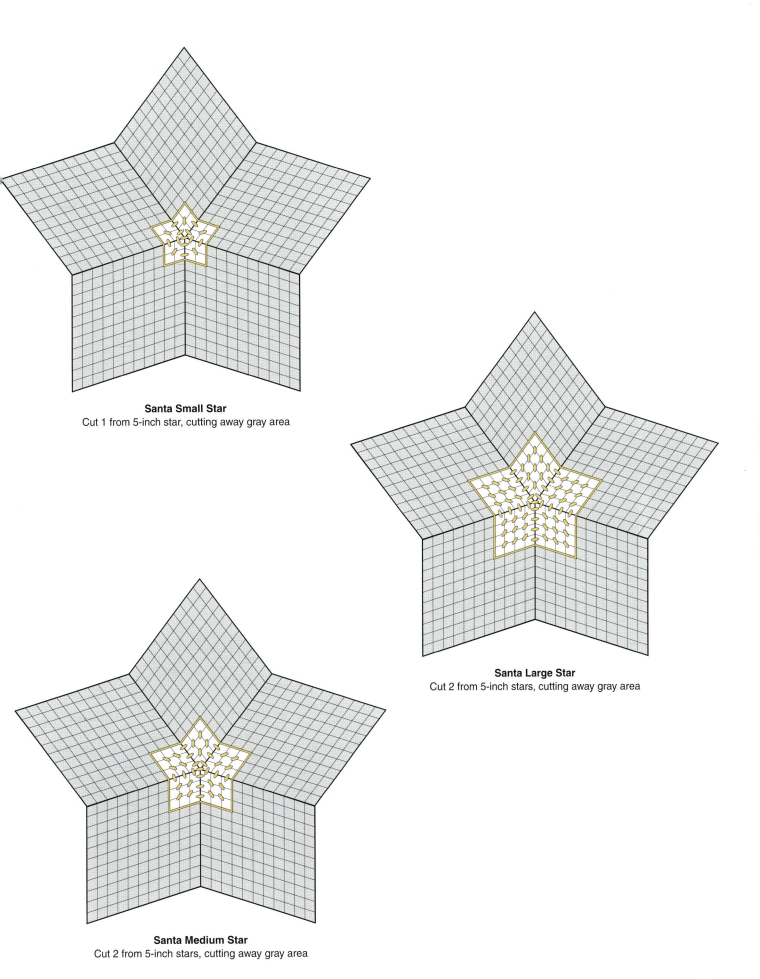

Textured Doorstop

Design by Celia Lange Designs

Size: 4¼ inches W x 7⅞ inches H x 2¾ inches D (10.8cm x 20cm x 7cm) excluding handle
Skill Level: Beginner

Materials
- 2 sheets Darice Ultra Stiff 7-count plastic canvas
- Red Heart Classic Art. E267 medium weight yarn as listed in color key
- Brick or other weight
- #16 tapestry needle

Stitching Step by Step

1. Cut two front/back pieces, two top/bottom pieces and two sides from plastic canvas according to graphs.

2. Stitch plastic canvas according to graphs, working purple and red sections first, then blue sections.

3. When background stitching is complete, work purple Straight Stitches on center blue sections according to graphs.

4. Using Olympic blue yarn throughout, Whipstitch front and back to sides at corners. Whipstitch top to front, back and sides.

5. Insert brick or other weight. Whipstitch bottom to front, back and sides.

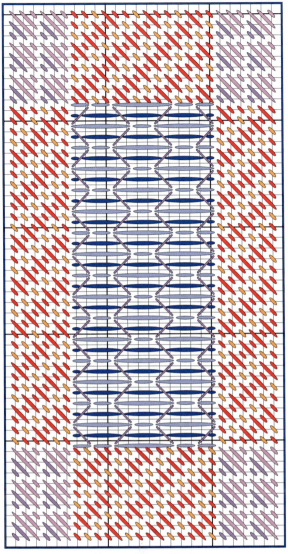

Textured Front/Back
27 holes x 51 holes
Cut 2

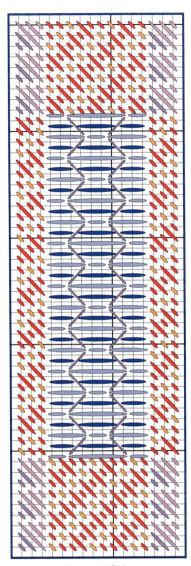

Textured Side
17 holes x 51 holes
Cut 2

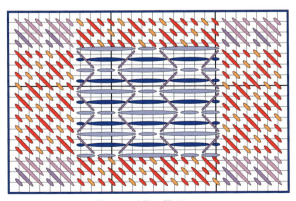

Textured Top/Bottom
27 holes x 17 holes
Cut 2

COLOR KEY	
Yards	**Medium Weight Yarn**
11 (10.1m)	Amethyst #588
15 (13.7m)	Purple #596
14 (12.9m)	New berry #760
18 (16.5m)	Skipper blue #848
18 (16.5m)	Olympic blue #849
14 (12.9m)	Cardinal #917
	╱ Purple #596 Straight Stitch

Color numbers given are for Red Heart Classic Art. E267 medium weight yarn.

Copyright © 2008 DRG,
306 East Parr Road,
Berne, IN 46711.
All rights reserved.
This publication may not be reproduced in part or in whole without written permission from the publisher.

The full line of The Needlecraft Shop products is carried by Annie's Attic catalog.
TOLL-FREE ORDER LINE
or to request a free catalog
(800) 582-6643
Customer Service
(800) 449-0440
Visit AnniesAttic.com

We have made every effort to ensure the accuracy and completeness of these instructions. We cannot, however, be responsible for human error, typographical mistakes or variations in individual work.

ISBN: 978-1-57367-304-4
Printed in USA

1 2 3 4 5 6 7 8 9

Before You Cut

Buy one brand of canvas for each entire project, as brands can differ slightly in the distance between bars. Count holes carefully from the graph before you cut, using the bolder lines that show each 10 holes. These 10-mesh lines begin in the lower left corner of each graph to make counting easier. Mark canvas before cutting; then remove all marks completely before stitching. If the piece is cut in a rectangular or square shape and is either not worked, or worked with only one color and one type of stitch, the graph is not included in the pattern. Instead, the cutting and stitching instructions are given in the general instructions or with the individual project instructions.

Covering the Canvas

Bring needle up from back of work, leaving a short length of yarn on back of canvas; work over short length to secure. To end a thread, weave needle and thread through the wrong side of your last few stitches; clip. Follow the numbers on the small graphs beside each stitch illustration; bring your needle up from the back of the work on odd numbers and down through the front of the work on even numbers. Work embroidery stitches last, after the canvas has been completely covered by the needlepoint stitches.

Shopping for Supplies

For supplies, first shop your local craft and needlework stores. Some supplies may be found in fabric, hardware and discount stores. If you are unable to find the supplies you need, please call Annie's Attic at (800) 582-6643 to request a free catalog that sells plastic canvas supplies.

Basic Stitches

Continental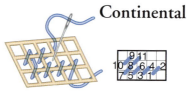

Overcast

Whipstitch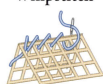

Slanted Gobelin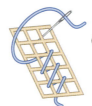

Long

Cross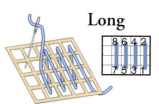

Embroidery Stitches

French Knot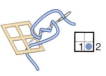

Lazy Daisy

Backstitch

Straight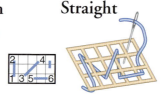

METRIC KEY:
millimeters = (mm)
centimeters = (cm)
meters = (m)
grams = (g)